— Reader 1

Stories for beginners

by D. Hilborne-Clarke and G. Heinrichs

Verlag Lambert Lensing · Dortmund

YES – A New English Course, Band 1
Additional texts for reading
(present tense)

Umschlaggestaltung und Illustrationen: Wolfgang Schütz, Weil der Stadt

ISBN 3-559-**75117**-9

Alle Rechte vorbehalten

© 1981 Verlag Lambert Lensing GmbH, Dortmund

Die Vervielfältigung und Übertragung auch einzelner Textabschnitte, Bilder oder Zeichnungen ist – mit Ausnahme der Vervielfältigung zum persönlichen und eigenen Gebrauch gemäß §§ 53, 54 URG – ohne schriftliche Zustimmung des Verlages nicht zulässig.

Satz und Druck: Ernst Knoth, Melle

5. Auflage 1987

TABLE OF CONTENTS

Grade 1

It's a dog's life 5
(making use of the vocabulary up to unit 6)

Helping the police 7
(making use of the vocabulary up to unit 7)

At the youth hostel 9
(making use of the vocabulary up to unit 8)

Grade 2

Spook's birthday party 12
(making use of the vocabulary up to unit 9)

At the department store 14
(making use of the vocabulary up to unit 10)

Chimpy's holiday 16
(making use of the vocabulary up to unit 10)

It's a dog's life

Bow wow. I'm King. I'm Dennis' dog. We live at 27 Church Street in Inverness. This is what I do every morning.

Bow wow. It's a quarter to six, time for a good dog to get up. John, his father, and his mother are in bed, but I get up at a quarter to six. Every morning at a quarter to six, that's King's time.

Then I go to Kitty. She's our cat. A stupid little cat, but she loves me. Her hobby is playing with me. She sleeps under Dennis' bed. Bow wow. Kitty opens her eyes, miaow. She gets up and then we go into the kitchen.¹ There's Miss Molley. Can you guess who she is? Dennis' sister? Wrong! She's our parrot. Parrots are stupid, but Miss Molley is nice. She's not from Inverness. I think she's from Africa. She can say "Kitty stupid" and "Dennis stupid" and "King, good boy". I think she likes me very much.

Then Kitty, Miss Molley, and me go back to Dennis' room and play with his bag, with his football shoes, or with his exercise-books. We hide his pencil-case under the table or in the cupboard in the kitchen or

---

¹ kitchen ['kitʃin] – Küche

in Kitty's box under Dennis' bed. Dennis always says "No", but King does what King thinks is right.

And where is Dennis? Schoolboys! He is in bed. Half past six – Dennis is in bed, seven o'clock – Dennis is in bed. Schoolboys can sleep and sleep, dogs can't.

It's a quarter past seven. Rrrrr! Dennis sits up in bed and opens his eyes. We all sit down on his bed until Dennis' mother comes and says, "Get up, Dennis, it's time for breakfast" and "King, Kitty, Molley! Come here! You can't sit on the bed." Kitty and Molley get up, then Dennis and then me, and then we go to the kitchen and have breakfast. After that we go into the garden[2], and I play with Dennis and with Kitty and Molley, of course.

At half past eight Dennis says bye-bye. He goes to school. School is only for boys and girls, I know, but Kitty and Molley always want to go with him. But he always says "No". That's right. What can teachers do with dogs, cats, and parrots? Nothing. What a stupid thing school is! So we are at home. We sit in the garden or in Dennis' room until Dennis is back from school at half past four. It's a dog's life.

---

[2] garden ['gɑːdn] – Garten

Helping the police

1 Old lady: 9 – 9 – 9. The police, please.
Police: Sergeant Stone. What's your name and address?
Old lady: I'm Mrs Christie of 33 New Street. I'm using the telephone near the Midland Bank[1] in the High Street.[2]
Sergeant Stone[3]: Thank you. What can I do for you, madam?
Mrs Christie: Something is going on at the bank. You see it's Saturday afternoon, and there's a big car standing near it and ...
10 Sergeant Stone: Yes, madam?
Mrs Christie: ... and there's a man and his friend, and now one of them is trying to get in.
Sergeant Stone: Trying to get in? Where? Is he trying to get into the bank?

[1] Midland Bank [ˈmidlənd·bæŋk]   [2] High Street [ˈhaistriːt]   [3] Sergeant Stone [ˈsaːdʒənt·stəun]

15 Mrs Christie:		Yes. And he has got on a mask,[4] I think. Yes, he has. He has got on a mask, and now he's taking something to the bank.
Sergeant Stone:		What is it?
Mrs Christie:		I think a bag and ... No, I can't see what it is.
20 Sergeant Stone:		O. K. Has he got a gun,[5] then?
Mrs Christie:		Oh yes, a gun. I think it's a gun. Yes, that's it. It's a bag and a gun.
Sergeant Stone:		O. K. Thank you. Now wait there and do nothing. We're coming now. And please do nothing. The man 25 has a gun. And the man in the car? Is he still there?
Mrs Christie:		Yes, he's waiting.
Sergeant Stone:		Thank you.

Two police cars come to the bank. The policemen know the gangsters have got guns. So they have guns, too. Three policemen get out and go
30 to the gangsters' car. They get the man sitting in the car. "Hands up," they say. The man puts up his hands and says, "Can't you read, boys?" "Read? You put up your hands, and no stupid talking." "Stupid? Who's stupid? Can't you read what's on the car?"

Policeman: Look at that, Sergeant.
35 Sergeant Stone: What? Where?
Policeman: On that car over there.

Sergeant Stone reads: BBC – TV.

---

[4] mask [mɑːsk] – Maske   [5] gun [gʌn] – Gewehr, Revolver

At the youth hostel

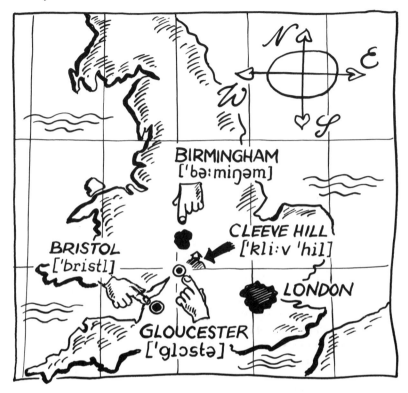

1 Stanley and Walter's class is staying at the youth hostel on Cleeve Hill near Gloucester. The class comes from Birmingham and is staying on Cleeve Hill for two weeks. It's nine o'clock at night, and the boys and girls are all in bed. The boys are trying not to make a noise. They know
5 that Mr Bull comes into their room at five past nine to see if they are all in bed.

Stanley:	Heh, what about Bob?
Walter:	I know. He still isn't here.
Stanley:	Ssh! Let's put his bag into his bed so Mr Bull doesn't see
10	that he's not here.
Steve:	Where is he then?
Walter:	He's out with Sheila.
Steve:	Sheila? Who's that?

	Jim:	A girl from Cleeve.
15	Stanley:	Ssh! Bully is coming.
	Mr Bull:	Are you all in bed?
	Boys:	Uhm.
	Mr Bull:	Good night, and no noise or there's no swimming or playing football tomorrow[1], but lots of work. You know
20		Maths is lots of fun.
	Boys:	But, sir, we're sleeping, we're not making a noise.

(*Mr Bull goes out.*)

	Walter:	Bob is an idiot. What can we do about him?
	Stanley:	Yes, no football or swimming until we get back home, and
25		lots of Bully's fun.

(*a noise at the window*)

	Steve:	Ssh! What's that?
	Walter:	Bully is coming back.
	Steve:	No, it's at the window.
30	Jim:	A ghost! Help! Bully's ghost!
	Steve:	Don't be stupid. Look at the window.
	Stanley:	I think it's Bob.
	Walter:	Yes, it's that idiot Bob. Open the window for him.
	Jim:	Don't make a noise. Bully is still not in bed.

35   (*The boys open the window.*)

	Steve:	Come in, you stupid idiot. Don't make a noise, or Bully ...

(*The door opens.*)

	Mr Bull:	What's this noise ...? Haha! Oh, it's you again, Bob Carter, or is it his ghost?
40	Bob:	Well, sir, uhm ..., no, sir ...

---

[1] tomorrow [tə'mɔrəu] – morgen

Mr Bull:	Now tell me, Carter. Where are you going?
Bob:	Well, sir, it's ... uhm ...
Mr Bull:	Going? Or is it coming? Let me see. What's that in your bed? A bag. Oh, I see. You're coming, Bob Carter.
45 Bob:	But, sir, Sheila and me ...
Mr Bull:	Aha! Back from the girls, Mr Bob Carter? Fun with Sheila today, fun with Maths tomorrow and tomorrow and ...

Spook's birthday party

1 It's Spook's birthday party. All his friends are with him. The door bell rings. Spook puts on his new school head, the present from Archie, and his new coat from Jolly Roger.
   "Who's that?" he says. "All my friends are here."
5 He opens the door. Whooosh! His three sisters.
   "Oh," says Spook, not very happy. "Who are you? You three can't come to the party. All Spook's friends are here, and we don't like girls like you."
   "Who's that?" Dolly asks her sisters.
10 "We don't know," they say. "Ask him."
   "Who are you?" says Dolly. "You look like a schoolboy. We can't stand schoolboys. They're boring and too young for us."

"And we can't stand you," says Spook. "Why are you here? You know Spook is having a party today. Where do you come from?"

"Oh, that's nothing for schoolboys. We come from the Black Ghost's bikini party. That's nothing for little schoolboys like you. You are much too young for dad and mum parties."

"O. K. then," says Spook. "Go back to your stupid old mums and grandfathers. This party here is great. No bikinis, but lots of cake and records. Much better."

"Hey! Who are you? Records? Cake? This is stupid! Where's Spook? Get our brother, you nosy little boy. We're Spook's sisters. You can't talk to us like that. Get Spook to the door, son."

Then there's a big noise. Jolly Roger and all Spook's friends come to the door. They want to know where Spook is.

"Oh no!" says Jolly Roger. "The three nosy, noisy, stupid, boring old sisters. What do they want?"

"They want to talk to Spook, but they can't find him," says Spook. "Aren't they stupid?"

"Yes. We all know how stupid they are," says Jolly Roger. "And awful and boring and . . ."

"Where's our brother Spook?" say the three sisters. "We want our brother now! This minute!"

"He's not here," says Archie. "He's at Edinburgh Castle."

"Edinburgh Castle? Why?"

"He's playing ghosts for Archie's grandfather. It's the old man's birthday today. He's 90 years old," Nessie tells them.

"Oh, stupid Spook. Why is he at a teenager's party? It's so boring at teenagers' parties. No bikinis, just a lot of boring guitars and dancing."

"Well, you go to Edinburgh Castle and ask Spook if you can come in here. This is his party. Tell him, if you come we go."

"Edinburgh? That's a long way. We want to ring Spook up."

"Well, you can't come in here and use Spook's phone. And we haven't the number in Edinburgh, too."

"No, we don't want you here. Go away. You're awful," says Jolly Roger.

The three sisters go away and Spook and his friends all laugh.

"What a great head this is," says Spook. "Now I can get away from my sisters after 500 years. They don't know me with this school head."

At the department store

1   It's Joan's birthday, and her friends Linda and Susan go into a big department store in Newcastle to buy a present for her. They don't know what to give her, so they want to look in a lot of departments in the store to get some ideas.

5   Linda: I know. Let's go and look at the scarves.[1] There are some nice red and black Scottish ones in the shop-window.
Susan: Oh yes, that's a good idea. They're on the third floor, I think.

(*The girls go up to the third floor.*)

10 Linda to salesgirl:
We want to look at the Scottish scarves. Where are they, please?
Salesgirl: They're over there near the cardigans, dear.
Linda: Thanks.

15 (*They find the scarves.*)
Susan: Oh, look, Linda. This one is lovely, and it's not very ...
Woman: Give me that. That's my scarf. I want it.
Susan: But we ...
Woman: I don't want to hear that. Give me that scarf, or must I get
20 the salesgirl?
Linda: Oh, give it to her, Susan. We can look at some other scarves.

(*The woman goes away with the scarf.*)

Susan: What an awful old bag!
25 Linda: Yes. But look! What's she doing? She's just putting the scarf in her bag and ...
Susan: Yes, and look! Now she's taking a blouse. Let's watch. There she is again. She's putting it in her bag.
Detective: Now, you two. What are you doing?
30 Susan: Doing? Why do you ask? We're just looking for a present.
Detective: Well, not playing, I hope. This is no place for playing and being noisy, you know.
Susan: But we only want to ...

---

[1] scarves ['skɑ:vz] – plural of scarf

Linda:	Oh, come on, Susan. Let's look at the T-shirts over there. Joan likes them, I think.
Susan:	O. K. But I think we must tell...
Linda:	Oh, come on, we don't know, do we? Look at this yellow T-shirt. It's great, isn't it? Susan? Where are you?
Susan:	Look, Linda. Look at that! Now that woman is putting that...
Detective:	Oh, that's it, is it? You two again. Still playing, and now making funny faces at ladies.
Susan:	Ladies? What lady? She isn't a lady.
Detective:	Now wait a moment. What's this all about? Do you know something?
Susan:	Yes, we do. Now...
Linda:	Oh, stop it, Susan. We don't *know*, we just *think*.

Susan:	O. K. then, Linda. We think that 'lady' is stealing² things.
Detective:	Stealing?
Linda:	That's right.
Susan:	You must look in her bag. Detectives can do that, can't they?

---

² to steal [sti:l] – stehlen

15

	Detective:	Oh, yes, I can do that. You're not playing funny games, are you?
55	Susan:	No. You look. There's a scarf in her bag, a blouse, and a pullover.
	Linda:	The scarf is red and black.
	Detective:	O. K. then. But you stay here and wait. I just hope you're right.
60		(*later*)
	Detective:	Well, you're good detectives. She's a thief[3], and the store wants to give you something worth £10 each.
	Linda:	Great! I want some records.
	Susan:	Yes, me too. And we want that lovely Scottish scarf for Joan.
65		
	Detective:	You can't have that at the moment. We need it for the police.
	Linda:	Oh, we still haven't got a present for Joan.

---

[3] thief ['i:f] – Dieb

Chimpy's holiday

1 Mr Clarke is a bus driver in Bristol. Lots of people have got cats and dogs, but Mr Clarke has got a monkey. His name is Chimpy. Mr Clarke likes Chimpy very much, but when he wants to go on a camping holiday, Chimpy can't go with him. Mr Clarke asks Tom and
5 Peggy to take Chimpy for two weeks. He knows they like him very much.

"O. K.", they say, "that's great, but we must ask Mum and Dad first. We can ask them when they come home from work."
"That's good," says Mr Clarke. "I hope they say yes because Chimpy
10 likes you very much, too."
"Well," asks Peggy, "what does Chimpy eat?"
"He eats a lot of oranges, bananas and apples, and please give him water every day. He likes white bread sometimes, and he loves cakes and ice-cream."
15 "Oh," says Tom, "that's a lot, isn't it?"
"No, please don't give him too much," answers Mr Clarke. "Give him one or two bananas and one apple or an orange and a piece of white

16

bread every day. And he needs three or four cups of water or milk. Of course, I can give you the money before I go if your parents say yes."
20 "What about cake and ice-cream then?" says Peggy.
"Well, only if he's good."

"Hey, Mum and Dad, good you're here. Can Chimpy come and live with us for two weeks?"
"Just a moment," says Mr Turner. "Why's that?"
25 "Well, Mr Clarke wants to go on holiday, and he can't take Chimpy with him."
"So he wants Chimpy to come here, does he, uhm?" says Mr Turner, "well, I don't know about that."
"But why not?" says Peggy. "Chimpy is a good boy, and he often plays
30 here."
"Yes, but he doesn't live here, does he?" says her mother. "What does he have to eat?"
"Oh, that's O. K., Mum," says Tom. "We know what to give him and how much. And we've got time to buy all the things he needs. We're
35 on holiday."
"Oh, you've got time, have you?" says Mr Turner. "And the money?"
"Mr Clarke gives us the money before he goes," answers Tom.
"So that's O. K. then, Dad?" says Peggy.

17

"Yes, but what about Tweets and Tiggy?" asks Mrs Turner.
"Well, that's not difficult. Chimpy knows them, and he likes canaries and cats."
"Yes, but where can Chimpy sleep?" asks Mr Turner.
"Well, you can take Tweets into your bedroom, and then Chimpy can sleep in a box in my room."
"And Tiggy? What about her?"
"Oh, she can stay in the kitchen," says Peggy.
"O. K. then," says Mr Turner. "I don't like it very much, but Fred Clarke is always friendly and is a good neighbour, so we can help him this time. But you do all the work. You get the money, you buy all he needs, you clean the room – everything."

It's the first day of Chimpy's holiday at the Turners. Mr and Mrs Turner are at work, and Tom and Peggy are playing with their three animals.
"I know, we can put Chimpy in the kitchen and see if he can find us in the bedroom," says Peggy.
"Great," says Tom. "Let's hide under the beds so it's difficult for him to find us." ...
"Tom, why doesn't he come? Do you think he can't find us? It's five minutes now. Do you think he's still in the kitchen?"
"Well, I don't know, do I? I'm under the bed."
"I know that, but what do you think, you idiot?"
CRASH! BANG!
"Oh, he's in the kitchen," says Tom.
BANG!
"The cups! Mum's best cups! He's not trying to find us, he's playing in the kitchen."
They run down into the kitchen.
"Oh, look! Three of Mum's best cups are broken! What can we do?" says Peggy.
"Well, we must go and buy three new ones before she gets home."
"What about the money?" asks Peggy.
"We must use some of Chimpy's money, and he gets no ice-cream and cake to eat."
"Oh, poor Chimpy," says Peggy.
"Yes, and it's poor us if Mum finds these broken cups. Let's put Chimpy in your bedroom, Peggy, and close the door. Then we can go and buy three cups."

18

"Oh dear, cups are expensive, aren't they? But we've got them. Chimpy can come out now," says Peggy when they get home again.
"Tom, Tom! Oh no! Look at this! My lovely posters!"
"What is it?"
"My posters! They're all in pieces."
"And look at your English book, Peggy. It's in pieces, too. And the bed. Look at the bed. It's all blue and red."
"And green. Felt-tips. Look, they're broken. Chimpy again," says Peggy.
"But where is he?" asks Tom. "Can you see him? Chimpy. Chimpy. He must be in here. Look, Peggy, the cupboard is opening. Who's that little girl?"
"Oh no!"
"Ha! Ha! Your lovely Sunday dress, Peggy, and your new bikini."
"You can laugh, Tom. Oh, Chimpy, you monster. You're awful. My posters, my felt-tips, and now my lovely dress. Come here. Chimpy, come here! Tom, get him! Stop him! Oh, no. He's away again. Where is he now?"
"I hope he's not in my bedroom," says Tom. "You know my model planes and records. Let's look."
"Well, you look under the bed, Peggy, and I in the cupboard. No, he's not here, is he?"

"No, he's not. I hope he isn't in the kitchen again."
"Yes, me too. But what's that, Peggy?"
PLOP! PLOP!
"Chimpy. No. The eggs. He has got the eggs, Tom."
PLOP! PLOP!
"Quick. Get him. That awful ..."
PLOP!
"Oh well, they're just eggs, Peggy. They're not so expensive as cups."
"Yes, but my dress. He has still got my dress on."
PLOP!
"Get him, Tom. Oh no. Now he has got the bottle of ketchup, and it's open. My dress, my lovely dress. Nothing but eggs and ketchup on it. I can never wear ..."
"Oh, come on, Peggy. You can wash a dress. It's not that bad."
"But we can't do it now, and Mum comes home in a minute. What can we do?"
"Well, get Chimpy first. Look, he's ... oh no ... the apple pie. He's sitting in it. So he has got his cake, hasn't he?"
"Come on, Tom, stop it. It's not funny now. Get that stupid little monster, put him in the bathroom, and close the door."
"O. K., then. I've got him. You begin cleaning the kitchen and ... Oh, hello, Mum."